Rosie and Mo went on the see-saw.

Sam said, 'I want a go.'

Rosie and Mo said, 'No!'

Rosie and Mo went on the swings.

Sam said, 'I want a go.'

Rosie and Mo said, 'No!'

Sam went on the climbing frame.

He went on the roundabout.

Rosie said, 'We want a go.'

Sam said, 'No! No! No!'

Then Mo saw Grandad.

Grandad said, 'I want a go.'

And everybody said . . .

'Yes! Yes! Yes!'